Milk

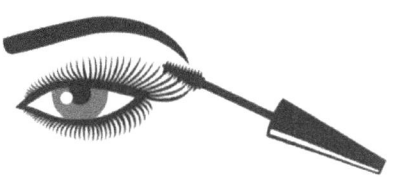

or

Mascara

A Collection of poems and tributes, inspired by life's little moments

Jeannette Angel

Copyright © 2024 Jeannette Angel

All rights reserved. No part of this publication may be reproduced, distributed, or transmitted in any form or by any means, including photocopying, recording, or other electronic or mechanical methods, without the prior written permission of the publisher, except in the case of brief quotations embodied in critical reviews and certain other noncommercial uses permitted by copyright law. For permission requests, write to the publisher, addressed "Attention: Permissions Coordinator," at the address below.

ISBN: 979-8-218-55012-7 (Hardcover)
Library of Congress Control Number: 2024950246

Any references to historical events, real people, or real places are used fictitiously. Names, characters, and places are products of the author's imagination.

Printed by DiggyPOD, Inc., in the United States of America.

First printing edition 2024

KLET & J LLC, Publisher
733 NE 204th St.
Shoreline, WA 98155

Dedicated to my sister,
Jennifer Angel-Lear
"Gone too soon"

Dedicated to my father,
Philbert James (Jim) Angel
"Also, gone too soon"

Table of Contents

The Hanky
61 Years
A Jingle for Santana
A Spit for G-Money
America Be Warned
America Lost
At This Point
Baseball Families
Beaver
Birdie, Birdie
Brave
Breakfast for G-Money
Budget
Clean Your Plate Club
Coffee Time
Complacent
Dads and Daughters
Denver
Diaper Rash
Empty Hand
Ethics
Falling Ceiling
First Lady
For Dan
For Susan
Here We Go Again
High School Football
History Made
Holidays
Hourglass No More
humpty trumpy
I Can't Believe
I Do
I Like Me
I Live
It's Raining
Jello

June 28th
Just A Steppingstone
Little Einsteins
Little Lamb
Making Memories
Maybelline Baby
Memories of a Hita
Milk or Mascara
Mister AG
Mom
My Bus Friends
My Country is Broken
My Daughter
My First Friend
My Fourth Grade Friend
My Mini Me
Nanny
Nikki Angel
Nikki Pooh
Not My First Lady
One Teardrop
Our Democracy
President Obama
Protect and Serve
Runaway
Scrambled Eggs
Second Place
Sick
Tea With Bea
Tears
Tents for Children
Tents for Children – Sequel
The Cult of trump
The Lady with the Blue Umbrella
The Letter C
The Marine
The Moon

The Prosecutor vs The Predator
The Vase
The Visiting Nurse
There are No Words
Ticker
Tiny Feather
Traveling Band
Turmoil
Uncle Gene
Uncle Uber
Us Through Each Other
Violence
Waddle, Waddle

We
We Remember
We Wait
Weeping Women
What Did He Know
What Once Was
What They Had in Common
What We Can Expect
Where Have the Republicans Gone
Yard Sale Blues
Yarn of Yesteryear
The Archives of My Mind

Foreword

I was so excited to share the title and some of the content of what I thought would be my first published book, with some of my favorite people; my longtime friends: Jeanne & Jerry, and Gwen.

We were meeting for brunch while Jeanne and Jerry were in town for a visit. They now live back in Utah after retirement.

Jeanne and I met in 1984, when I traveled to Utah on my first business trip while working at Mountain Bell. She was a supervisor in the accounting department, and I was the Methods and Procedures subject matter expert for her area of responsibility.

Jeanne rapidly became my "work Mom", so that made Jerry my "work Dad", even though he did not work with us. I met Jerry on that first trip. Jeanne invited me over for dinner on the first night of my trip. We enjoyed pizza and beer while getting to know each other. Jerry reminded me so much of my dad, so I immediately liked him. Jerry had the same work ethic and love & care for his family that my dad had for his family. I gained great respect for Jerry over the years. Jerry even drank the same brand of beer as my dad drank.

I feel so blessed to have worked with Jeanne as a peer and to have her as one of my many bosses over the span of my twenty-six-year career. Jeanne was one of my greatest mentors and her support for me has always been appreciated. I love you, Jeanne!

Gwen was another one of my mentors and bosses while I was, "Growing Up in the Phone Company". (a future book) Shortly after Gwen arrived, I whipped out my title page and proudly held it up for all to see.

"My View of the World"
"A collection of poems, tributes, and short stories, inspired by life's little moments."

Gwen turned to me and looked me directly in the eyes and said, "So! Who are you? Why would I want to read your book?"

Jeanne shot Gwen a look that I know Gwen has seen many times over the years. Gwen responded, "What! You know I have always been Jeannette's biggest critic."

True, Gwen is one of the brilliant women that I have worked for, she has always encouraged me to reach higher and dig deeper to accomplish goals. Some, I may have not even known I wanted to accomplish.

Gwen had such faith in my ability to lead that she promoted me to the Denver Database Administration team. I had no technology skills as a database administrator (DBA), but Gwen said the team preferred a "people manager" over a "technical manager." My predecessor was a technical manager, and the staff thought that he was too deep in the weeds. They wanted more freedom to do the technical work themselves.

I made it my mission to learn as much as I could about the job to be able to support my team. I was able to secure the necessary funding for training and tools, so we could provide the excellent customer service our clients deserved.

My position as DBA Manager was one of the most fulfilling positions of my career. I was proud of the team I started with and the team I built while I was in that position.

Once brunch was over, I went to a nearby bookstore, to browse the book titles. I picked up the books that caught my eye and grabbed my attention. I studied the color of the covers and the illustrations. I left the bookstore knowing that Gwen was right! My title was boring and just not a book even I would pick up. I wouldn't even give it a second glance.

The next morning, as always, I was talking to my cousin Bellina, while I was waiting for my bus. For some reason, Bellina remarked that I do not wear much makeup. My response was, "Well, when I go to the grocery store, I say, "milk or mascara - I choose milk!" We both laughed and then I boarded the bus.

I believe in signs, and I kid you not! I cannot make this stuff up! As I boarded the bus, I see a young woman sitting with her purse open on the seat next to her, loaded with makeup. The young woman was applying MASCARA! This was the sign I was looking for!

I sat right behind this woman, as the bus was beginning to roll off. I tapped the woman on her shoulder. She turned to look at me, with her mascara brush in one hand and her compact mirror in the other hand.

I started to ramble, "You are probably going to think that I am weird, but I believe in signs, and right before I got on the bus I was speaking to my cousin on the phone about milk and mascara."

Yes, she did look at me as if I were weird, but I kept on rambling. "I am writing a book and I am searching for a title, seeing you put on mascara has just convinced me that the title of my book will be, "Milk or Mascara - a collection of poems and tributes inspired by life's little moments."

The young woman said, "Well, I am not much of a reader, but if I saw that book, I would probably pick it up because I would be curious."

BINGO!

That was the reaction I wanted and the one that I believed Gwen was expecting.

The Hanky
by Jeannette Angel

I cannot remember a time
When I did not see my Dad with a handkerchief
"The Hanky"
He always has one handy
To wipe his brow
Or blow his nose
Or give it to one of his kids or grandkids
When they have a tear that needs drying
Or a runny nose
I can see my dad mowing the lawn and stopping to wipe his brow
He pulls the hanky from his back pocket
I remember when I was about eleven or twelve
I took up ironing
My Mom gave me a pile of hankies to iron for Dad
I got the iron steaming hot
Ironed out all the wrinkles
Folding the hanky in half and then in half again
I remember
The hanky was the size of a piece of
American cheese
I would stack those hankies
In a tall tower
Until they fell over
Then I would put them in Dad's drawer next to his socks
My Dad is not a rich man
But I wanted his offspring
To have a piece of him
Once he passed away, to that lawn in the sky
So, his hankies that I ironed so carefully,
I gave to all his kin to wipe a tear
Or blow their nose
Knowing Dad was always near

61 Years
by Jeannette Angel

Sixty-One years of Marriage
Some years full of Wedded Bliss
Some full of Wedded Blisters
Vows of for Better or Worse
Have been the cornerstone of this relationship
Growing old together
Walking hand in hand
Not always in lockstep
But ending up on the same road
Time and time again
No matter the quarrel
No matter the spat
They share the same bed
as they turn out the lights
Morning brings a new day together
Coffee is brewed
Toast is buttered
Celebrating the Love
They have for one another

A Jingle for Santana
by Jeannette Angel

Mr. Santana, sing me a song
When you are singing my heart beats strong
When you are singing, I sing along
Mr. Santana, please will you sing me a song

Mr. Santana, read me a book
When you are reading you get that look
The look of excitement, the look of a wise man
Mr. Santana, please will you read me a book

Mr. Santana, show me a dance
When you are dancing, I clap my hands
When you are dancing, I tap my toes too
Mr. Santana, please will you show me a dance

Mr. Santana, show me your smile
Your eyes are twinkling all the while
My love is growing with every grin
Mr. Santana, please will you show me your smile

A Spit for G-Money
by Jeannette Angel

My name is G-Ma
And I used to pull rank
Now, I'm poor with no money in the bank
I once rolled up in my Navigator
Now, I stroll so I'll get there later
RTD is my ride now
I sit and ponder and wonder HOW
My name is G-Ma
My Grandson's G-Money
He shoots the hoops, intercepts passes, and throws the rock
G-Money's all about action and not just talk
My name is G-Ma
With fourteen grandkids,
Some are big, some are small
Much love for them all!

America be Warned
by Jeannette Angel

Independence is at stake today
Our democracy has been challenged
The DOJ will determine
Who is and who is not
Above the law

Our Constitution was tarnished
And torn
When trumpsters stormed the Capitol

America be warned

Congressional hearings
Are underway
Witnesses have been sworn
To tell the truth
While under oath
Some have taken the fifth
Some are refusing to speak at all

America be warned

The world is watching
Will they see the fall of a Nation
The greatest Country on Earth
Or will they see
America the Beautiful
And Justice for All

America be Warned

America Lost
by Jeannette Angel

America Lost

America Fell

Half The Country

Has Marched U.S.

Into Hell

Just Wait And See

A New Reich

To Be

America Lost

The World Will See

A Democracy Crumbles

Here At Home And Overseas

Our Veterans Fought

So America Could Lead

But Today America Bleeds

At This Point
by Jeannette Angel

He wished for snow and
Asked for a joint
It was all he wanted
At this point

He said he had no pain
Always a smile
On his face

He was just waiting
To get out of this place

His brothers were waiting,
His Mother was too

He missed his twin
Like no other
Except for the loving arms of his Mother

He will ask his Father
Why did you leave us so young
We made do
But life wasn't the same
Without you

He misses his twin
How long has it been
More years in Heaven
Then here on Earth

Soon he will be reunited with his twin
Who he once shared a crib, a home, friends and family
Seeing his brothers again will bring him the joy of snow
And a high greater than the joint
At this point

Baseball Families
by Jeannette Angel

Fathers and Coaches
We're all team Moms
Our boys become brothers
Thicker than blood
We spend weekends at tournaments
Weeknights at practice
Under the lights
We travel to fields near and far
Our cars are loaded with all, of our gear
Cleats, gloves, bats, balls, uniforms
And coolers full of food
Barely enough room for our baseball players
And their biggest fans
Ball caps, not on heads
Roll around on the floor
When we get to the field
Our boys spill out of the cars
Morning games can be tough
If there was a sleep-over the night before
Once, our boys, step onto the field
They become Major league
Warmups, stretch, run, play catch, pump each other up
Into the dugout, they run
Toss a handful of seeds or a wad of gum into their mouths
Grab a bat
"Let's do this", they say
We sit in the stands, ready to cheer
Wishing for home runs
Knowing a walk is as good as a run
Get on base
Is our collective goal
Be ready to slide, steal second base
The Umpire signals
SAFE
We high-five, we are anxious for more
The sun beats down
This is perfect baseball weather
Spring, Summer, and Fall
Winter brings indoor practice
Baseball is a year-round sport for us
Our boys grow up before our eyes
Sharing gloves and bats and caps
Loving team Moms
Their Coaches and Dads
Baseball families are a tight-knit group

Beaver
by Jeannette Angel

That's my name
"Huh, Dad"
He would say
With pride in his voice
Grandpa would nod his head
In agreement
Grandma bought him a t-shirt
Printed with
Those very same words
She gave him that nickname
While he was still a baby
Nibbling on his wooden crib
And because
"Leave It, To Beaver"
Was a popular TV show
And Theodore was both their given name
As the years went by
Some called him
Beav
He took pride in his middle name
Which was, James
Same as his
Gramps
He went by Jimmy Angel
But to me he will always be
Son

Birdie, Birdie
by Jeannette Angel

Birdie, Birdie
Go back to sleep
I'm not ready to move my feet
Yes, I hear you chirping in the tree
But
I still have
Dreams to dream
And
Snores to snore
Birdie, Birdie
Go back to sleep

Brave
by Jeannette Angel

Do I go
Do I stay
Do I have what it takes
To endure another
Day
We are born
We live
And then we die
Is it my choice to say goodbye
Or do I leave that to happenstance
Should I give this life I lead
One more chance
Can I change my circumstance
Am I brave enough to venture on
Or am I braver to travel beyond
Will anyone miss me when
I am gone
Does it really matter
I am in control
We are born
We live
And then we die

Breakfast for G-Money
by Jeannette Angel

Monday through Friday
She's up at five
She makes my lunch
For my 9-5
Breakfast burritos
She hands me as I walk out the door
One for me and one for my ride
What I can say
About my grandma
Is she ain't no jive

Budget
by Jeannette Angel

365 days later
Waiting for a budget
Which has made our country broken
The White House
Is in chaos
No one is in the lead
Bannon was kicked out
Now we have Miller
Which could be worse
The world is watching
As we march in droves
They see our resistance
Of those in our House
Especially the one who
Believes he is a dictator
But in reality
He is just a pawn
Pawn of his staff
Pawn of Putin
Congress needs to step up
And take back our House
Can't they see
That the foundation is crumbling

Clean Your Plate Club
by Jeannette Angel

Grandma's club was easy to join
There was no fee
There were no dues
The only rule was to clean your plate at every meal
We all found that so easy to do
Melted butter on hot tortillas, such a treat
Wish there were more we could eat
Calido was her specialty dish
Licking the bowl was our only wish
Torte de huevos, smothered in red chili, another favorite
Tempting our senses of smell first, then taste buds dancing with joy
No one was excluded from this prestigious club
No membership card was needed
Come in, sit down, bow your head
Give thanks for the food you were about to receive
At the end of the meal if your plate was clean
President title was yours to hold
This title was more precious than gold

Coffee Time
by Jeannette Angel

Wake Up
Get out of bed
It's to the kitchen
Is where I head
I need coffee
I need cream
First thing in the morning
I don't want to scream
Fill up the pot
With cold water
Freshly ground beans
Smell so good
Just can't wait
For the brewing to stop
Take my cup from the shelf
Take my cream from the fridge
Stand at the counter
Staring at the pot
Drip, Drip, Drip
Now the last drop
Pour my first cup
The best of the pot
Add the cream
Take the first sip
Now, I can shout
"It's Coffee Time!"

Complacent
by Jeannette Angel

What happens when we all become complacent
What happens when we all say,
"I don't care"
"It doesn't affect me"
What happens when we don't speak up
When we don't speak out
We might as well not speak at all
When we do point out a wrong
Will anyone listen
Will anyone act
Will accountability be held
Will justice be served
What is there to lose
Self-respect
One's own dignity
Are these worth preserving
Am I my brother's keeper
Or is that just an ancient
Myth

Dads and Daughters
by Jeannette Angel

Dads and Daughters
Right from the start
Each captured one another's heart
He was her first hero
She, his very own Princess
He made her giggle & laugh when they played Peek-a-Boo
She made him so Proud when she graduated high school
His arm she held on so tight
When he walked her down the aisle
Her hand he reluctantly gave
To a man that could never take his place
Grandpa became his next moniker
Mommy became her new name
His eyes twinkled when he gazed upon his very own Princess
And realized she had become Queen of her very own Castle
Her heart swells with Pride every time she reminisces
Of all her Daddy ever did and ever said
What she has learned from him will never be forgotten
They hold hands for the very last time
She kisses him goodbye
As she sends him to his
Home in the Sky

Denver
by Jeannette Angel

Denver
My hometown
Now a big city
We can barely move around
Traffic at every hour
Everyday
We used to drive for twenty minutes
To get from door to door
Now lucky to be there in an hour or more
Denver natives are being pushed out
Transplants tout gentrification
While pouring our morning brew
The landscape is changing
And the skyline too
With this rapid growth
More and more are being left behind
Incomes have not risen
As fast as housing costs have climbed
Many more homeless
Then ever before
Parks and downtown sidewalks
Is where the homeless gather
In my hometown

Diaper Rash
by Jeannette Angel

I like a dry butt

I cannot lie

You don't want to be

poopie

And neither do I

Change my diaper every chance you get

No more diaper rash you can bet

It doesn't matter if it's Huggies or Luvs

Pat me dry

Before you

Secure my fly

Here is my handle

There is my spout

Hear me out

I like a dry butt

I cannot lie!

Empty Hand
by Jeannette Angel

Drugs
The Dealer
The User
Supply and Demand
One without the other
Is an empty hand
Hands that can be used to cradle a baby
and to hold a toddler's chubby fingers
as she takes her first steps
Hands that can be used to hold a book
while reading a bedtime story
or used to splash water while bathing the baby boy
Hands that can be used to caress a loved one
or cook a family meal
Hands that can be used to pray
for
a dried-up supply
and a disappearing demand

Ethics
by Jeannette Angel

Ethics
Where have they gone
By the wayside
I am afraid
What happened to morality
Can't find it in the workplace
Can't find it at home
Jiminy Cricket chirps all alone
No one will listen
No one cares
We have become the land of
Me
I am the only one that matters
Can't you see
No respect for the Elders
What do they have to offer
Their time of integrity
Gone with our greed
Leave me alone
With my coffer
It's the only thing I need
Ethics and Morals
Who needs
these

Falling Ceiling
by Jeannette Angel

She opened the door
She took the heat
She inspired us
To move our feet
She may have cracked the glass
She knew the cracks would not last
One day
That glass ceiling
Will surely
Fall
The breakthrough will be glorious
Madam President
For us All

First Lady
by Jeannette Angel

First Lady
Full of grace
Radiant smile upon her face
Uplifting messages she conveys
First Lady
Full of grace

First Lady
Standing tall
She demonstrates she loves us all
Growing her garden
On the White House lawn
Nourishing our stomachs, minds and hearts

First Lady
Making History
Never forgotten, always welcome
Grateful we are for all that she's done
First Lady
She will be missed

For Dan
by Jeannette Angel

Sitting in my favorite chair
early in the morning
The only sounds are the chirping birds
on my front lawn
And the clock tick-tocking on my kitchen wall
As I pick up my coffee cup
I get a glimpse of my snarly, wrinkly hands
After I sip my morning brew and set the cup down
I begin to examine my own two hands
First the left where my wedding band is tightly fit
As it has been for many, many years
I see the veins popping out slightly more than I recall
I look at my right hand in the very same way
Inspecting the wrinkles and callouses that I hadn't noticed before
What do these hands say about
How I have lived and worked and loved
Do they tell a story that I am proud of
As I stare at the these very old hands
My mind starts to wonder of the years, that have slipped by
I remember when my hands were smooth as silk
When I caressed the cheek of my first love
Hard work with a mop and a broom
Then paint brushes, shovels, and rakes
These tools were hard on my hands
And callouses they made
But these hands are what kept my family fed
As I turned my hands over and over
From palm to knuckles
I could feel the first time that
I turned a key in the ignition, and gripped a baseball bat
I could feel my little one's hand
Cupped inside of mine
When I walked him to school on his very first day
These hands opened a lot of doors
And slammed a few shut
Many a handshake and pats on the back
Yes, these hands have experienced that
High fives and knuckles
With teammates and friends
Boy, these hands have done a lot
Touched a lot of people over the years
These hands of mine have prepared plenty a meal
and always are clasped when saying Grace
I pick up my cup
The coffee is cold
But I have two strong hands
To make a fresh pot

For Susan
by Jeannette Angel

Oh, sweet Mama of mine
You held me tight when I was young
You watched me run
You picked me up when I would fall
You said to soar
I did so with a roar
Now I hold you tight
I watch as you take
Your final flight
Kiss my Dad
Hug my Brother
Oh, sweet Mama of mine

Here we go again
by Jeannette Angel

What did he know
When did he know it
January 6th
Was a planned event
Death to democracy
Was the goal
What did he know

Little by little
Bit by bit
Information is emerging
He knew
The plan
He created
The plan
He called
His henchmen
He called
His flock

March is what he said
Fight like hell
Is what he yelled
Stop the counting
Stop the certification
Stop the peaceful transfer of power

Take the Capitol
Take the ballot box
Take the VP
And Madam Secretary
As well

Storm, they did
Havoc they wrecked
Chaos they bestowed
What did he know
He knew it all

High School Football
by Jeannette Angel

Walking down Louisiana Avenue
Passing the park
Admiring the leaves as they turn
From green to gold
Any day soon it will be cold
Only branches left, to hold the snow
Walking down Louisiana Avenue
On my way to the stadium
To watch Geno play
What a great evening for football
Air is crisp with a fall breeze
Hoping to see the Vikings
Bring Kennedy to their knees
A hope not fulfilled
Kennedy beat the Vikings
By quite a few
Walking down Louisiana Avenue
No more smile upon this face
Can't win them all
Still, it is painful to watch the
Vikings fall

History Made
by Jeannette Angel

History Made
That's what she said
With pride so sincere
Tears of joy run down our faces
As our hearts swell and beat
For those who came before us
And for those that will come after
Madame President
Sounds so good to hear
18 million cracks
But still not broken
The fights not over
We have just begun
As we still struggle to be
One nation where there is
Liberty and Justice
For All

Holidays
by Jeannette Angel

Christmas came
Christmas past
Looking forward to the
New Year
What will be
We will see
Happiness and grief
Failure and healing
One day at a time
Valentine kisses
Spring break
Summer fun
Autumn leaves
School bells ring
Halloween treats
Giving thanks once again
Christmas has come

Hourglass No More
by Jeannette Angel

I have not grown old gracefully
From my head to my toes
I realize my youthful appearance
Is a vision of the past
Why or why can't physical beauty last
My hair is thinning and to the touch
It feels like Brillo
Cream rinse and conditioners fail
To smooth and shine
Yesterday's mane is no longer mine
At one point in my youth
An hourglass figure was mine to behold
Now it's hard to describe the shape
I see in the fitting room mirror
Not a square or a pear
Maybe multiple balls of blubber and fat
More than one spare tire as a matter of fact
As a young woman, I never imagined that
Wow!
My legs once shapely
Were my best attribute
Years of walking have increased
The size of my calves
No longer worth looking at
But, in this, day and age
A complement of one's shapely legs
Is no longer a compliment
But a vulgar remark
Complements of beauty have
Become a thing of the past
If I think that my legs
Are no longer my finest asset
I can't even begin to describe
The worst of the worst
It pains me to say this
More than my shoes hurt my feet
Once high heels were my greatest desire
Every heel length from gorgeous short pumps
To four-inch heels
I stomped around daily
And danced in them too
Now flats are the kindest gift
I can give these creature-like toes
No, I have not aged gracefully
But thank God every day for the opportunity to age

humpty trumpty
by Jeannette Angel

humpty trumpty
Sat on his wall
Let's just watch our Democracy fall
He called all. of his henchmen and
Said.
Nancy and Schiff will never put it together again
I have Putin
I have Mitch
If the Dems aren't careful
Barr and Miller will push them in a ditch
I have Rudy - he did jest
Rudy spins a story - he's the best
humpty trumpty
Sat on his wall
America and the World are waiting for his
BIG
Fall

I Can't Believe
by Jeannette Angel

Standing in the hallway
Calling out
"anyone home"
Oh, no
I think that I am all alone
My dad just left me
My mom's not here
Oh, Dear
I can't believe that this is happening to me
I think that I should go find help
Mrs. Neighbor
Are you there
It's raining and I am scared
Oh, no
I can't believe that this is happening to me
I see a light at Megan's house
Her mom will know what to do
Knock, knock
Can I come in
Oh, my
Yes, dear come right in
Let's get you dry
Let's get you fed
We'll wait for your mom
She'll be here soon

I Do
by Jeannette Angel

Today we say
"I Do"
Today we become one
We have been a couple for a while
Just this morning we awoke as engaged
Tonight, we go to sleep as
Mr. and Mrs.
How special is that
Newlyweds we will be for at least a year
Maybe two
Once we settle in as husband and wife
A twinkle in the eye
Will become a bundle of joy
The years will pass
Our love will grow
And celebrations of
"I do"
Will be toasted annually
How happy and content we will be
Year after year
Married life will be good to us
I am so glad that today we said
"I Do"

I Like Me
by Jeannette Angel

I like me
I am smart
I am strong
Sometimes I am wrong

I like me
I am loyal
I am diverse
Sometimes my life goes in reverse

I like me
I am fun
I am funny
Sometimes I wish I had more money

I like me
I am creative
I am caring
Sometimes I am daring

I like me
I make memories
I am happy

I Live
by Jeannette Angel

I gather trash
I cook meals
I leave the light on for my girls
I load the dishwasher
I fold the towels
I watch my grandkids
Play in the snow, read books, build Lego towers
And play computer games
I dust
I scrub the tub
I inquire about your day, your mood, your health
I sweep
I shovel
I love your laugh and your company
When you take the time to visit
I work
I create
I live for mine and theirs

It's Raining
by Jeannette Angel

My pants are soaked
My hair is frizzed
It is what it is
It's raining

The car broke down
All I can do is frown
It is what it is
It's raining

My kitchen pipes are still backed up
Fix the car or fix the pipes
It is what it is
It's raining

Still have a part-time job
Looking for another
It is what it is
It's raining

No money in the bank
All the bills unpaid
It is what it is
It's raining

The weeds keep growing in the yard
Can't afford a gardener
It is what it is
It's raining

I need a loan
I can't repay
Just waiting for a Sunny Day!

Jello
by Jeannette Angel

Counting down the days
Because
now I know
what I did not know
A Year Ago

Twenty-Eight days
I had left
with the most influential man
in my life

My Dad

Father's Day
He was celebrated
Like every other year
He sat on the patio which
He and his brothers'-in-law
And his friends had built
Surrounded by his family who adored him
He was able to hold the youngest of the bunch
And mouth
"Grand Pa"
As he had done for all that came before

Jello was served in his honor
As the little ones have always clamored
"Jello"
As they ran to the kitchen
Knowing Grandpa
Always has Jello in the fridge

Grandpa knew the little ones
Would ask for his special treat
Not popsicles or ice cream
Did they want to eat
Jello
And Jello alone was what they would
Come to know as
Grand Pa!

June 28th
by Jeannette Angel

June 28th
That was the date
Dad said,
He just couldn't wait
He took his last shower
He took his last walk
This was the date of our last talk
He asked for his family
He asked for the Priest
He asked for his sisters
He was ready to meet
His Heavenly Father
and to reunite with his
Baby daughter

Just a Steppingstone
by Jeannette Angel

VP
Is just a steppingstone
We all know
She did not get there alone
Strong Women
Supporting
Strong Women
They have paved the way
From coast to coast
Laid every brick
Drank from the
Black and brown fountains
Picked grapes, lettuce, and cotton
From fields and plantations
Strong Women
They have planted the seeds
In the hearts of Strong Women
Not willing to sit
In the back of the bus
Rosa
Sat in the front
She sat there tall
Ms. Johnson, Ms. Jackson, and Ms. Vaughan
All aimed for the stars
And the orbit above
If they could work for NASA
If Maxine could fight in the Congress
Then Harris
Can work for the people
In the White House
VP
Is just a steppingstone!

Little Einsteins
by Jeannette Angel

Vinny and JoJo are brilliant
Little Einsteins from the start
Yearning for knowledge simply leaps from their hearts
Reading, writing, and arithmetic are not subjects they just learn in school
Reading, writing, and arithmetic are fundamentals of their future
Just the tools
Science and technology, subjects that they love
Science and technology, subjects that they excel in
So easy to get excited when they look up above
The planets and the stars not far from their reach
One day, one of them may travel to Mars
Math bees and Science fairs challenge them today
The universe may challenge them down the road
Master Chef, Astronaut, Computer Scientist
Dreams to behold
All is possible when learning is important
Questioning and curiosity are encouraged and expected
Little Einsteins from the start
Such pride, flowing from my heart
Vinny and JoJo are Brilliant

Little Lamb
by Jeannette Angel

My Child
My Son
My Little Lamb
My Heart was joyful
The day you were born
My Heart swelled with Pride
Every day that you lived
My Heart broke into a million pieces
The day that you died
My Heart beats slowly
With each Decade I pray
For the Little Lamb
Returning home
to the Loving Arms
Of his
Father

Making Memories
by Jeannette Angel

Making memories with my grandchildren
That's how I spend my days
I would not have it any other way
Each one holds a special place in my heart
Each one loved immensely from the very start
Seven are girls
Seven are boys
What they bring me is pure joy
Talents they each have are plenty
Interests they are exploring
Amaze me greatly
Their futures are still ahead of them
Grounded in what came before them
Memories of today will always surround them
What did Grandma say
What did Grandma do
Remember when, Oh Yes, we do
She gave us space to explore
She gave us opportunities we can't ignore
She loved us unconditionally
She supported us enthusiastically
In her eyes we were superheroes
There is nothing we can't accomplish
Making memories is her goal
When she is gone this is the only gift
She can bestow
Memories, more precious than gold
Memories that can't be sold
Memories are her daily goal

Maybelline Baby
by Jeannette Angel

The golden ringlets framed her creamy, China-doll face
Her eyelashes appeared to be covered in mascara
So long and so full
Those eyebrows of hers
Were thick with a perfect arch
I called her my Maybelline baby

One day we were waiting in line
At the checkout stand
I heard a gasp from behind me
I turned around
A woman was looking at
No
Staring at my sweet little girl
"She is so beautiful: she literary took my breath away"

I said,
"Thank you, she has the same effect on me"
Her eyes are mesmerizing
Her smile melts hearts
A sweeter voice
I have never heard
So silky smooth when she decides to sing
Such a gift, I did receive
On Labor Day morn

Memories of a Hita
by Jeannette Angel

Oh, mi hita
She is so beautiful
What will her name be
Thank you, Auntie,
Maybe Bella, Maybe Mia
Maybe I'll name her Hita
Oh, mi hita
She is growing so fast
Look how she laughs
When I tell her "quack, quack"
Auntie, you are so funny
Thank you
for giving her that bunny!
Oh, mi hita
She is walking and talking now!
She is so sweet
Thank you, Auntie,
She is what makes my heartbeat!
Oh, mi hita
It's hard to believe, she is in kindergarten
Before we know it, she will graduate high school
Imagine then, what she will do
Her singing and dancing
Will take her far
Yes, Auntie
I agree
Mi hita
Keeps me busy
With her dance classes and her music programs
She is my shining star
Oh, mi hita
Look at your Hita now
Up on that stage
Microphone in hand
Hear everyone clapping
See that they stand
Oh, Auntie
I am so Proud
Yes, I hear the clapping
It is so very loud
Watch my Hita
She is taking a Bow

Milk or Mascara
by Jeannette Angel

Milk or Mascara
Not a hard choice at all
Beauty budget or office supplies
Not a hard call
No blush or eyeshadow
Left in the drawer
Chapstick instead of lipstick
No money for more
A made-up face
Or a plain Jane
The difference between
The Haves and the Have Nots
Milk or Mascara
The choice of the poor

Mister AG
by Jeannette Angel

No Person is above the law
We will see
Mister AG
Insurrectionists
Created the coup
What will Mister AG do
Attempt to overthrow our government
Interrupt our peaceful
Transfer of power
Where is Mister AG
Not too far
No Person is above
The Law

Mom
by Jeannette Angel

She was a bride at seventeen
GG at seventy-eight
You only have one Mother
Dad would say
She has only one job
To go to the beauty shop
And to be beautiful
He said that too
Her heart was broken at a very young age
When God took her firstborn
He was a beautiful baby boy
Not even a month old
She raised five other children
One boy and four girls
Her heart would break even more
When God would take her lastborn
Her beautiful baby girl
Even though Jen was only 41
Mom's favorite song is
"Smile"
Sung by Nat King Cole
It sums up her philosophy
She is so strong
Her hobbies are sewing and gambling
Her favorite number is nine
Not only is she a great Mother
She is a great Mother-In-Law as well
She will never meddle
But if asked
She will give wise advice
Mom is a good cook
Even though she doesn't like to eat
She taught my brother
How to make green chili and tuna casserole
And how to stand on his own two feet
She was a bride at seventeen
Married most of her life
Her husband may frustrate her at times
But he also makes her laugh
Which is the answer she will give when asked
How she stayed married for so long
"Jim makes me laugh"
She will say with a smile on her face
My Mother's beauty is more than skin-deep
Many times. I have wished
I was more like her
But Mom taught me to be me

My Bus Friends
by Jeannette Angel

We chat to and fro
Nice to see you
How was your day
It's hot today
Looks like rain
How about those Broncos
Did you watch the game
I didn't see you yesterday
Were you sick
No, just a day off
Took my dog
To the Vet
Any plans for the weekend
Do you date
Oh, here is my stop
See you tomorrow
Have a nice night
Glad we could talk

My Country is Broken
by Jeannette Angel

My Country is broken
My heart is too
Whatever happened to the
Red, White, and Blue
Treason
Is becoming commonplace
Day by day
It is in our face
The Supreme Court
Has no restraint
Making it easier for
ONE
To
Reign

My Daughter
by Jeannette Angel

She's my Daughter
She will never be replaced
She went to Heaven
To see His face
He welcomed her into his warm
Embrace
She rested her head against his chest
I heard my daughter whisper
Thank you, Father
For tucking me into bed
Where I can
Rest

My First Friend
by Jeannette Angel

My Brother
Jim
How can I ever thank him
For all he's been
My first playmate
My first ally
He shared his toys
He shared his parents
The bond we have should never end
My big brother
My first friend
As we grew
He walked me to school
He made me laugh
He made me cry
He played practical jokes
That made me mad
But then he would laugh
And so, I laughed too
I can never stay mad
At my first friend
As we grew up
We remained close
Both a bit wild, but in different ways
He drove cars, fast
I grew up faster
I had a kid
He became an uncle
His support has never wavered
My brother Jim
My first friend
As we grow older
We always have a shoulder
He confides in me
And I in him
He still makes me laugh
Rarely do I cry
He still plays practical jokes
I don't get as mad
I love him unconditionally
I think he is strong
I think he is kind, most of the time
He has integrity
He speaks his mind
My big brother, Jim
My First Friend

My Fourth Grade Friend
by Jeannette Angel

My fourth-grade friend
She was a straight A student
I was just as smart
She was tall and lanky
I was short and spunky
She was fascinated with makeup
I was fascinated with boys
We rode the bus to Junior High
Where many a grade school friendship ends
We remained close
Through seventh, eighth and ninth
Not a better friend, I could ever find
High school arrived and she began to drive
She tried to teach me on her standard shift
But stopped the lessons before
I could blow her clutch
Her high school years were full of
Fun and folly
This left her a few credits short
She went to summer school to get her diploma
I went to work to support my kids
My fourth-grade friend went to several colleges
Until she found her calling, she became a lawyer
I worked for a corporation
It wasn't long before she became famous
A bid for Mayor, she did that too
I am so proud of my fourth-grade friend
Decades of life's experience we have shared
Childhood crushes
Births, weddings, family deaths
Divorces, mine, not hers
Purchases of our first homes
Holiday celebrations and vacations too
My life has been enriched
By loving
My fourth-grade friend

My Mini Me
by Jeannette Angel

My mini me
That's what we called her
Her hair was dark and curly
She was so tiny
Just as I had been
She has grown into a young lady
Finding her way in the world
A nurse or barber
For her profession
Which will she choose
No matter which one
She will be successful
Her work ethic
She has already proved
I am so happy to have her
In my life
Excited to see how she matures
No matter how old she gets
Or how successful
She will always be
My Mini Me

Nanny
by Jeannette Angel

Being a Nanny
Best job of my life
A thousand times better than
Being a Wife

Picking up toys from the floor
Just so the babies can throw some more

Changing diapers
Wiping noses
Smelling baby feet
Which smell like roses

Teaching these young minds
ABCs and One, Two Threes
Nursery rhymes
And telling time

Greatest job in the world
Not a job at all
Being a Nanny
Makes me feel ten feet tall

Nikki Angel
by Jeannette Angel

"Nikki Angel"
"Come on down"!
Grandpa shouts from his favorite living room chair
I run down the hall
And stop right next to him
As he points to the TV and shouts
"What is the price of the TV"
"And if you get it right"
"A Brand-New car!!"
I scream as I jump up and down
Clapping my hands
And spinning around
Grandpa laughs while stomping his feet
As he often does
His dimples get deeper with every grin
This is the game we play every day.
It never gets old
Bob Barker and Grandpa
Are laughing up a storm
As Grandpa tells Bob

"You are the next contestant, on The Price is Right"

Nikki Pooh
by Jeannette Angel

Who knew
What a wonderful
Woman
You would grow into
With your head on straight
With such a warm heart
Where did the time go
Watching you accomplish your goals
Was heartwarming to me
Wishing you Joy, Love & Happiness
Will always be my thought
Well, you have become the
Best Mom
Best Wife
Best Friend
Nikki Pooh
Who Knew
Love Mom

Not My First Lady
by Jeannette Angel

Not my first lady
No, not at all
Not even to her husband
Number 3
If I recall
Not my first lady
Either she is ignorant
Or just doesn't care at all
Do U
Not my first lady

One teardrop
by Jeannette Angel

He doesn't always hit me
She says,
While standing at her kitchen sink
He doesn't always hit me
She says,
While lowering her head
Just, as I catch a glimpse of two blackened
Eyes
Fading beneath
Smudged caked-on face makeup
He doesn't always hit me
She says,
As one teardrop falls
From her left eye

Our Democracy
by Jeannette Angel

Our Democracy
Is too important
To hand it to a fool
Who is just a puppet to a few
It's not only Putin
Who pulls his strings
It is maga, who kisses his ring
Beware of Project 2025
And
Agenda 47
Written for the Puppet
And his sidekick, JD Vance
Behind the scenes are the dangerous villains
Of the Heritage Foundation
And a list of boogiemen standing
At our bedroom doors
And our doctors' offices too
Fiery torches they hold in their hands
To burn the books, they have banned
WOKE up
This morning to the sound of drums
VOTE, VOTE, VOTE
Was the beat that moved my feet
Knock on doors, make some calls
Please don't let our democracy fall
VOTE BLUE
Up and down the ticket
Don't give our Country to the
Wicked!

President Obama
by Jeannette Angel

President Obama
He served us well
Such a shame, not all could tell
He served with dignity
He served with grace
All the while, a smile on his face
His Presidency was a first
Since the Nation had its birth
A black man in the lead
Yes, he led
Yes, indeed
Moving forward, chopping at the debt
Taking down Bin Laden
Without regret
Diplomacy was his approach
Some condemned him with reproach
Healthcare for his countrymen
At the top of his list
Affordable thought to be a myth
Selecting a Justice was his duty
Congress failed to vet his choice
Protesting his selection
Sitting on their derrieres
Such a shame his hands were tied
Leaving the court an empty chair
Who would think that this was fair
Eight years have come and gone
Leaving him a little grayer
Leaving him a lot wiser
President Obama
He served us well

Protect & Serve
by Jeannette Angel

Protect and Serve
It's not just a job description
It is their life
In and out of uniform
It does not matter
Protect and Serve
Is in their blood
It is more than bravery
That drives them
It is their duty
They have sworn
May they be the Men and Women in Blue
Who patrol, our streets
or may they be the Men and Women
In the US Armed Forces
Who fight, for our freedoms
And protect our Constitution
These Men and Women
Deserve our respect
And our appreciation
They Protect and Serve
The RED, WHITE, and BLUE

Runaway
by Jeannette Angel

Runaway, Runaway
Why do you run
Where are you running to
Where are you running from
How may I help you
What can I do
Will you run forever
Or just for a year or two
Are you looking for someone
Are you looking for you
Are you looking for answers
Where in the world would you find them
Are they here at home
Maybe you really, don't have to roam
Runaway, Runaway
Where will you go
How long will you be gone
How long do you plan to stay away
Will you miss us
Will you call
Will you even think of us at all

Scrambled Eggs
By Jeannette Angel

Sizzle, Sizzle
In the pan
Yes, we hear you
Yes, we can
Scrambled eggs
We do make
For our breakfast
We can't wait
Yummy, yummy
Scrambled eggs

Second Place
by Jeannette Angel

Second place is no disgrace
We played hard to keep the pace
They played harder and won
First place
We never gave up
We took all our shots
We hustled up and down the court
But when the buzzer went off
We were a few baskets short
Our fans cheered us on
Until the very end
Watching the clock tick down
As our adrenaline ticked up
Our heads knew there could only be one winner
Our hearts believed it should be us
Not this game, the scoreboard showed
Second place is no disgrace
Especially when it's the championship game
Looking back at all the games we have already won
Knowing we are Champions
Number One
In the hearts of our families and teammates
Holding our heads up high
Yes, second place is no
Disgrace

Sick
by Jeannette Angel

I need Mucinex or
Claritin-d
I should drink orange juice and
Some hot tea
My head is pounding and
My nose is stuffed
Sick on vacation
Just my luck
Get me some Kleenex
Where is the Tylenol and
My shawl
I can't get out of bed
Not for a minute
Not at all
I need to feel better
There is so much to do
I want to go a visiting
but
Here I sit
Boo Hoo

Tea with Bea
by Jeannette Angel

I never imagined
I never knew
That I would be asking
One lump or two
To our former First Lady of Colorado
Mrs. Bea Romer
The tea was English Breakfast
There were scones with jam
And honey
This was more than a tea
It was a fundraiser and an ask
For money
The race was for Mayor
Of the city of Denver
It was a run-off
Between Chris Romer and Michael Hancock
My candidate of choice
had lost the primary race
So here we were
Having tea with Bea
Mrs. Mejia and Theresa's mom, Joan
Were also sipping tea
In the Romer home
Three previous rival camps
Had come together
But, tripling the team would not overcome
Hancock
He was elected Mayor in 2011
It wasn't so bad
As it kept Denver blue
It was an honor to ask
One lump or two

Tears
by Jeannette Angel

Tears, tears
So many tears
Tears of joy
Throughout the years
Tears of sorrow
That feed our fears
When our hearts are broken
Our eyes weep with tears
that run down our cheeks
Are they meant to cleanse the wound
We feel may never heal
A really, good cry
A flood of tears that clear the mind and soul
And light our spirit
These tears may not be welcome
but
Surely needed
Tears, tears
So many tears
A single teardrop
As significant as a sob
Depending on the person
Tears behind closed doors
As important as the ones that flow in the open
Tears of Happiness
Tears of Sadness
All are meant to show emotion
Love, Compassion, Anger Joy, Heartache, Triumph
Tears, tears
So Many Tears

Tents for Children
by Jeannette Angel

Tents for children
Not for play
Meant to house until the day
Customs comes to take them further away
Brownsville now
Tornillo next
Why not trump tower
For their heads to rest
Is it because these children are not from Sweden
Is it because they migrate from the South
South of the border they travel
With families who love them
Where are the parents
Border security put them
Behind bars
Zero tolerance is a Session's mantra
It separates children from their Ma and their Pa
Department of Homeland Security
Has been tasked to snatch these children
And snatch them fast
Health and Human Services
Are put in charge of these tent shelters
And the children of immigrants
Who have become
Lost
This practice of this administration
Is not human at all
This practice is cruel and unusual punishment
Of the weak and the small
No matter your party
No matter your religion
This practice is not American
No, not at all

Tents for Children
The Sequel
by Jeannette Angel

Just when I thought
This couldn't get worse
I see that bond has been denied
No matter that the Judge
Has ordered to
Reunite
This administration is putting up a fight
The children are hurting
They cry through the night
We all can see
This isn't right
Now a form, parents must sign
Go home with your children
Or go home alone
This inhumane behavior
Of Sessions and trump
Is making a mockery
Of our democracy
Of Lady Liberty's creed too
Never again can we hold our heads high
When we have stooped this low
This separating of children
From the arms of their parents
Is a crime more dangerous
And wrong
Then crossing the waters and climbing a wall
How much further does America have to fall
Before Congress tells this Administration
To Go to Hell

The Cult of trump
by Jeannette Angel

The Cult of trump
Where did they come from
How did they grow
Americans now reap what they sow

Thousands upon thousands of lies
Accumulated and became
The Big Lie
The Cult of trump
Took this to heart
They drank the Kool-Aid
Which poured from trump's
Mouth

The Cult of trump
Marched from the deep
To the top of the hill
Where they would spill
The blood of democracy
And the Officers charged to guard it

"Hang Pence"
They shouted with fists in the air
This call was heard near and far
The Cult of trump
Followed the words of their leader
trump gave them the courage
To interrupt and destroy
Democracy
On that cold January day

The Cult of trump
One by one
Arrested, tried, and convicted
Jailed and fined
Where is their leader
Not far behind

The Lady with the Blue Umbrella
by Jeannette Angel

The Lady with the Blue Umbrella
Trudges through near knee-deep snow
To get to the bus stop
To and fro, she goes morning and night
Snow, rain, sleet, and sunshine
Just like the mail carriers
She passes from time to time
This is her path
One she has made over this last year
But really a path she has made over her lifetime
She trudged through the hills and valleys of her life
Just as she does today
Through the hills and valleys of the snow
Made by the wind, crafting drifts as high as her thigh
And valleys as low as the soles of her boots
Ten minutes ago, she was standing in a valley in her dining room
Counting out enough change for three bus fares
She had to borrow sixty cents from her baby grandson's piggy bank
This really, is a new valley for her
Even though she didn't put an IOU in the bank
The IOU is in her head
Which will be paid in full, with interest too
The lady with the blue umbrella is grateful
For her life path, even the valley she is in now
With every valley, there is a hill to climb
The lady with the blue umbrella is searching for her next hill
With the same excitement, she imagines one would have
When beginning the climb of Mt. Everest

The Letter C
by Jeannette Angel

Collusion
Conspiracy
Coordination
Cooperation
All begin with the letter C
Crime
Crackdown
Conviction and Cell
They begin with the letter C as well

Can you tell

I have been playing with Santana's Christmas gift
of magnetic letters, we have on the refrigerator door

The Marine
by Jeannette Angel

He was a Marine
In an Era when it was
Unpopular to be a Marine
He fought in an unpopular war
If ever there was one
He endured conditions to him
Were unfathomable
Alongside men who would become his lifeline
And he would become theirs
The jungles were full of leeches
They clung to his clothes and his skin
The jungles were dense and dark
Wet and laden with the enemy
Was this what it meant
To serve his country
This question was asked, there in the jungles
And at home
He served with Honor
He made it home
When others did not
He survived the Hell
If anyone deserved to live
It was He
The Marine

The Moon
by Jeannette Angel

What's your favorite object in the sky
The moon, I say
But why
No reason, just asking
What about those stars
So bright and shiny
Scattered about the night sky
Don't you like the way they twinkle
Sure, I do, but still not my favorite
Luna
Is my favorite and will always be
Especially when it is full
No wait
A Harvest Moon
To see the orange glow
Makes me happy
I could stay up all night
Just gazing up at the
Man in the Moon
Well, how about those planets
Jupiter or Mars
No
The Moon is my favorite

The Prosecutor vs The Predator
by Jeannette Angel

The Courtroom
Is
Every rally stage
In
Every state
Across the USA
The Jury
Of his peers
They are listening
With all ears
Closing arguments
Will take place
On the
Debate stage
Deliberations
Being held
Around every kitchen table
From the East to the West
From the North to the South
The Verdict
Comes down
On
November 5, 2024

The Vase
by Jeannette Angel

The Vase
Holding up and supporting the beauty
Of the Rose and the Daisy
For all the world to admire and celebrate
The Vase
A vessel for the water
Which gives the Rose and the Daisy
Nourishment to stand strong
and Bloom
The Vase
The Rose
And the
Daisy
Giving the world
Happiness and Joy
As they share the same space

The Visiting Nurse
by Jeannette Angel

The visiting nurse came today
She said,
It's almost time for you to go away
You won't be far
As you will always be in your loved ones'
Hearts and minds and thoughts
The visiting nurse came today
She took my pulse and my blood pressure
As she always does
She smoothed my blankets
And washed my face and body
With the gentlest of care
She noted my chart
And spoke quietly to my family
Who had gathered on this day
She said,
It's almost time
For your loved one to go away
I could hear the cries and the sobs
And a little tear
I too shed
Not for me
But for them
As I know I wasn't going far
My mark, I had already made
In the hearts, minds and thoughts
Of the ones that have gathered all around me
On this day, that the visiting nurse had come
As I lay here in my room
My life really does pass before me
And I am ready and happy to know
It won't be long before my Lord
Will come to carry me home
I am thankful
The visiting nurse came today

There Are No Words
by Jeannette Angel

There are no words
That I can say
To convey
How sad
I am for you today
My heart is aching
As yours is breaking
There are no words
To explain
This cruel moment
That will linger on and on
In every passing second
Of every day
In every passing year
There are no words
That will leave my mouth
And touch your ears
That will
Comfort you
There are no words
Only arms to hug you
And shoulders to give you
While
There are no words

Ticker
by Jeannette Angel

A heart is more than just an organ
It is the center of one's soul
It is where one holds another dear
Especially when they are not near
A heart is more than just an organ
It is a universal symbol
Of love and valentines
Of thine
Even when a heart is broken
It will continue to tick on
Because
A heart is more than just an organ

Tiny Feather
by Jeannette Angel

The first Easter
Since you floated home
You sent a little sign
Telling us that you are fine

A tiny little feather
Floated down from Heaven
It was white as snow

The tiny little feather
Floated down from Heaven
And rested on the kitchen counter

I was browning the roux
And right there and then
I knew
Tiny little white feathers
Float
Down
From
Heaven

To carry your love and affection
To those you left on earth

Happy Easter!
Happy Easter!

Traveling Band
by Jeannette Angel

Strike up the band
Play a happy tune
Trombone, Trumpet
Someone play the spoons
Shall we march in a parade
Or make music in the
Orchestra hall
Either one is just as fun
For this traveling band
Bring on the drums
And the saxophone too
We just love
Making music for
You

Turmoil
By: Jeannette Angel

This is a time of turmoil
No time to be complacent
The Constitution is our Rule
Why did we hand it to such a Fool?
We are the land of the Free and the Brave
Not an Island to ourselves
Global economy is a must
That's the way to keep the Trust
Freedom of the Press is what keeps us Honest
"Alternative Facts" are just lies to Con Us
Bans and mass deportations are not the Answer
Building walls will not Advance Us
No time for Political Rift
What we need is Political Shift
A little to the Left
A Little to the Right
45's Administration keeps me up at Night!

Uncle Gene
by Jeannette Angel

He was a Chiropractor
He was a Dad
He was the only
Husband she ever had
He loved his family
He cared for his patients
He respected his colleagues and his profession
He was a fan of the Broncos and the Rockies
His hometown teams
He was a man of God
His faith never wavered
He was a tall man
He had a great laugh
He was loved
He was admired
He will be missed
He was
Uncle Gene

Uncle Uber
by Jeannette Angel

Uncle Gary, was his name
Until he landed in Denver
Then Uncle Uber, he became
He didn't realize that he would drive
From sunup to sundown
All around his old hometown
Actually, he crossed a few county-lines
In his short time here
He drove North, South, East and West
Wow!
Uncle Uber
You're the best
He drove kids to school
Which wasn't that far
He really, did like driving
Auntie Angie's car
Not to worry
It won't be long before
Uncle Uber
Is chauffeured back to DIA
But who should we ask to take the wheel
The "Old People" or
One of his favorite nephews
We love you
Uncle Uber!

Us Through Each Other
by Jeannette Angel

Looking at the ocean through his eyes
Fills me with wonder and surprise
Seeing the clearest blues and foamy whites
Loving the ocean with all its sights

Listening to the waves through his ears
Continues to amaze me through the years
Hearing them crash against each other
Before rolling softly upon the shore

Feeling the mist of the sea upon his face
Sprays of water I can trace
Patting the wetness with my loving touch
Right before I kiss him
This Man I Love So Much

Looking at the Mountains through her eyes
Fills me with wonder and surprise
Seeing the forest through the trees
This beauty brings me to my knees

Listening to the wind through her ears
Continues to amaze me through the years
Hearing the rustling of the leaves in the fall
And the howling when winter comes

Feeling the warmth of the Sun, upon her face
Welcoming rays of sunshine highlight her Grace
Touching her glistening cheek
Right before I kiss her
This Woman I Love So Much

Violence
by Jeannette Angel

Violence
Violence
Everywhere we turn
Shootings from sea to shining sea
Homegrown killers wreaking terror
On us, one and all
Nothing a ban or wall
Could prevent
Disenfranchised, mentally unstable
Non-believers in the American Dream
What can be done to stop the madness
Take our healthcare
Take our services
Tax the middle class
Make the rich wealthier
This can't be the answer
Public servants
Have you forgotten
We the people
Who, you have sworn to serve
Stop the greed, and self-serving
Stop the ignorance and the inexperience
Return our country
Or amber waves of grain

Waddle, Waddle
by Jeannette Angel

Lately, I have noticed
That when I get out of bed
I waddle to the kitchen
When I used to glide instead
I drink my morning coffee
So, I can clear my head
Getting ready for my day
Thinking about how the hours fly
And how the years are slipping by
I'm not afraid of getting old
I'm young at heart you see
This is my intention
To always be
Waddle, Waddle
So happy to be me!

We
by Jeannette Angel

Do we stand
Do we kneel
Do we condemn
Do we praise
Do we judge
Do we curse
Are we Americans
Are we free
Are we brave
May we protest
May we disagree
May we serve
May we support
We do stand
We do kneel
We do condemn
We do praise
We do judge
We do curse
We do protest
We do disagree
We do serve
We do support
We are free
We are brave
We are Americans!

We Remember
by Jeannette Angel

Today, we remember
We remember their laughter
We remember their smiling faces and twinkling eyes
We remember their walk, their run, and their stance
We remember their scent which still lingers in our hearts
We remember their kiss goodnight and kiss hello
We remember their first day of school and
High school graduation or that college diploma
We remember the way they slipped that ring
Around our finger on our left hand
We remember how gently they cradled our babies
We remember our song and our first dance
We remember their promise to return home safe
We remember that they
Served

We Wait
by Jeannette Angel

As we sit and Wait
Here in the Land
Of the somewhat Free
And the sometimes Brave
We Wonder
Will our Democracy Fall
Or will our Constitution
Prevail
We the People
Deserve to have our Voices
Heard
No matter if We
Have cast our Vote
Blue or Red
Democrat or Republican
The Counting
Must
Continue
Once all our Voices
Have been Recorded
Tallied
And Announced
We will have the Answer
For which
We
Wait

Weeping Women
by Jeannette Angel

For all the weeping women
Yes, I cry with you
You are not alone
I am your home

For all the weeping woman
I know your heart is broken
Just remember
You are not alone
I am your home

For all the weeping women
I will carry you
When you are not able to walk alone
I am your home

For all the weeping women
I am here for you
To tell a joke or two
I will make you smile
I will make you laugh
You are not alone
I am your home

What did he know
by Jeannette Angel

What did he know
When did he know it
Unanswered questions
Have become a habit
Digging for the truth
Is a fulltime job
Alternative facts are
Becoming the norm
The Special Council
Needs to Separate
The dirt
Well before the Constitution
Is permanently hurt

What did he know
When did he know it
Did he collude
Was it treason
Follow the money
Thirty-years in the Making
Deals with the Russians
With family and friends
Just waiting to see
How this all
Ends!

What Once Was
by Jeannette Angel

Sunshine and Little Sunshine
He called us for such a short time
His eyes twinkled when he smiled
My heart melted from within
I still miss him to this day
And wish him blessings along his way
I am proud to have loved him
He is such a good man
Many a lesson he taught our boys
Integrity, honor
How to win
And more importantly
How to lose
Some grew up
And followed in his footsteps
Coaches they became
His three sons I am sure
Are proud to carry his name
People come into our lives for a reason
For us, it was only a season
Memories of our time together are bittersweet
Mostly tucked away until the skies turn gray
And the wind begins to blow
Reminders of that November trip
To the dock of the bay
Returning home with souvenirs
Still not tarnished, despite the years
I have no illusions that what was once
Will ever be again
I am just giving thanks for what was
No matter the reason

What They Had in Common
by Jeannette Angel

What they had in common
They were both fathers
And they were my good friends
I respected them for the lives they chose
And the bravery that they showed
I never knew the pain they were in
Not even at the very end
They both had smiles that lit up the room
It was my pleasure to work with them
They never let me down
Our projects were always successful
I wish their treatments had been too
It was in the early days
Not many would survive

What they had in common
Was what they had to hide
HIV and AIDS you see
Were not acceptable diseases
It was a different time
People were in fear

What they had in common
Is within my heart
They will always be near

What We Can Expect
by Jeannette Angel

Deflection
Deception
What he does best
Look over there
Don't look here
There is nothing to see
Flip and flop
A game he plays daily
Just to conceal his hand
Name-calling and demeaning
The best of the best
Just to hide what is under his vest
Chaos and confusion
In this house of cards
Who will pick up the pieces
Once it all implodes
Incompetence is the highest level of experience
We can expect
Until this administration is put to rest

Where Have, The Republicans Gone
by Jeannette Angel

Where or where have the Republicans gone
Where or where have they gone
Turning their backs
Closing their eyes
So they do not see
The carnage laid at their feet
Plugging their ears
So they do not hear
Cries coming from the streets
Keeping their mouths shut
Not speaking any dismay
For their leader's hateful
Racist remarks
Directed at people of color
From south of the border
And across the seas
Where or where have they gone

Where or where have the Republicans gone
Where or where have they gone
Talk of socialist behavior
Coming from the right
In order, to mask and hide
America's fight
With the NRA
America's fight
Against communist behavior of
The current regime
Holding court in the Oval
Where or where have they gone

Where or where have the Republicans gone
Where or where have they gone
Not one in sight
Not one with courage
Not one with desire
Not one to get in the ring
Not one to expose
He was never a Republican
Where or where have they gone

Yard Sale Blues
by Jeannette Angel

Yard sale blues
Is what we have
Set up early
With coffee in hand
Not a buyer in sight
Until half past ten
A ninety-four-year-old man
Who just wanted to talk
And the neighbor down the street
Who just stopped to gawk
Iced tea we offered to the little old man
He appeared parched
After an hour had passed
Half past two
We greeted a few lookie-loos
Nothing impressed them
Not even the brand-new shoes
Cracked open the beers
Just about three
Then sat under the shade
Of the front yard tree
To sip a few
What else can you do
When you have the
Yard Sale Blues

Yarn of Yesteryear
by Jeannette Angel

Melinda, here is a skein of yarn
Light purple for my newest baby
Granddaughter
Will you crochet her a crib blanket
Oh yes, I will be delighted
No rush
Oh, the yarn of yesteryear

Melinda, where is the crib blanket
I gave you that purple skein of yarn
The baby shower was last month
Oh, I am sorry
I will get it done

Melinda, Ari is now one year old
She won't be in a crib much longer
Do you still have the purple yarn
Yes, I do
But where did I put it
Oh, the yarn of yesteryear

Melinda, Ari started kindergarten
What color was that yarn I gave you
Oh my, I think it was purple
But I just can't find it
Melinda, never mind
Ari is a big girl now
With a comforter for her bed
No wait!
I found the yarn of yesteryear
Yes, it is purple
Not enough for a bed
But extra yarn I can add
Ten years later
A crocheted bed throw
Made with Grandma Joanie's purple yarn
By Auntie Melinda
Who added yarn of her own
Made just for Ari
Made with love
With yarn from yesteryear

The Archives of My Mind
by Jeannette Angel

Traveling down the archives of my mind
What do I see
What do I find
In this archive of mine

There, I go hand in hand
With my first friend
Off to school
Just a block or two
I was four
My sweater was blue, my blouse was white
Mama watched
I knew because I turned to wave
I see her walk back to our cracker box house
I see this in my archive mind

Traveling down the archives of my mind
What do I see
What do I find
In this archive of mine

Grandma Nora and Auntie Esther
Curlers and pins in their hair
Mama roasting turkey
Daddy resting on the couch
In our little cracker box house
I see this in my archive mind

Traveling down the archives of my mind
What do I see
What do I find
In this archive of mine

Grandma Sadie lives next door
She has a cracker box house of her own
Uncle's yellow car is parked in the front
The grass just mowed
We all run from Grandma's lawn to our own
I see this in my archive mind

Traveling down the archives of my mind
What do I see
What do I find
In this archive of mine

We left the little cracker box house
Moved into a house on a hill
grape vines and shade trees that's what I see
George once played hide and seek with me
He babysat us, just once
In our house on the hill
I see this in my archive mind

Traveling down the archives of my mind
What do I see
What do I find
In this archive of mine

We made friends with our neighbors
While living in the house on the hill
We walked our dog, Chain
Actually, he walked us
I see this in my archive mind

Traveling down the archives of my mind
What do I see
What do I find
In this archive of mine

Again, we moved when I was a kid
From the house on the hill
To the home where my parents live still
Dad planted a tree
A blue spruce
It started out in a coffee can
Now it towers over the house
Where the Angels reside
Until God calls us home

Acknowledgment

A special Thank you to my Publisher, Gary M. Trujillo, my Editor, Nicole Angel Mendoza, Don Trujillo my Artistic Designer and all my family and friends who inspire me everyday to write about life's little moments.

www.ingramcontent.com/pod-product-compliance
Lightning Source LLC
LaVergne TN
LVHW061526070526
838199LV00009B/389